WHY A Better BE

Beth Fiedler

Copyright © 2014 Beth Fiedler

ISBN: 978-0-9920937-4-7

All rights reserved. No part of this book may be reproduced or transmitted in any form or by any means, electronic or mechanical, including photocopying, recording, or by any information storage and retrieval system, without permission in writing from the copyright owner.

This book is presented solely for educational and entertainment purposes. The author and publisher are in no way liable for any misuse of the material. Although the author and publisher have made every effort to ensure that the information in this book was correct at press time, the author and publisher do not assume and hereby disclaim any liability to any party for any loss, damage, or disruption caused by errors or omissions, whether such errors or omissions result from negligence, accident, or any other cause. References are provided for informational purposes only and do not constitute endorsement of any websites or other sources. Readers should be aware that the websites listed in this book may change.

This book was printed in the United States of America.

DEDICATION

This book is dedicated to my parents, my siblings Eva, Teresa and Leung, my husband Nelson and my best friend Terry, whose support and love continues to inspire me to live to the fullest and share what I have learned.

ACKNOWLEDGMENTS

I thank my husband, Nelson, for once again sharing the journey of developing a book with me. I thank him for his continued patience and support when I lost myself in writing and publishing activities.

I thank my parents for a special childhood. I learned from them and will always remember who and what they were.

I thank my siblings, Eva, Teresa and Leung, for the valuable memories we created together.

I thank my best friend, Terry, who has always been there for me.

I thank my Toastmasters peers, Andy, Irene, Pony, Alfred, Barnabas, King, Talis, Philip, Angela, Daisy, Joeie, Paulise, Queenie and Susan (plus many other devoted Toastmasters), for their enthusiasm and committed support of the Toastmasters movement in Hong Kong.

I thank my people managers and mentors, Walter, Tim, Amy, William, Andrew, Vincent, Gerry, Frances, Brugh, Clint, Drew, Robin and Marc, for their guidance and insightful suggestion.

I thank my long-time friends, Teresa, Anita, Candy, Helen, Sannie, Ivy, Eva, Karen, Ming, Marion, Salina, Alice, Johanna, Linda, Landa, Alan, Drew, John, Stephan, Glenn, Louis, Siu, KK, Stella, Choy Gor and Ting Je, for their continued presence in my life across space and distance.

I thank my friends, associates, partners and customers, whom I am fortunate to know and work together, for their open, honest and supportive sharing of ideas and feedback.

I am grateful for the opportunity to share my learnings with you.

CONTENTS

INTRODUCTION

Appreciation	1-4
Dream	5-10
Etiquette	11-16
Growth	17-26
Happiness	27-30
Inspiration	31-42
Love	43-50
Relationship	51-60
Time	61-66
Wellness	67-78
Core Values	79-82
Biography	83-86
Glossaries	87-88

INTRODUCTION

We do not get explanations in life. Most of us may choose to go with the flow and seldom ask why and how can we make the same experience differently next time.

In this book, I wrote about common things that are part of our daily lives. These common things and words make me tick. I share my ideas and how I react to them. It is not my intention to preach what is right or wrong.

We are all different. What inspires me might bore you. The differences between us are not relevant. What is important is for you to be able to take a step back, analyze yourself, and answer the Why questions. For example, "Why and What You Are?", and "Why you are who you are?".

This book could be my biography because it captures what is important to me and my philosophy.

My father passed away when I was six. I had a distant relationship with my mother who became a single parent of four when she was only 30.

Bits and pieces of our daily trifles have been the precious moments that stay with me. I still remember who and what my parents were decades later.

Most parents are trying to teach their children manners and important life lessons they learned themselves. Will their children remember what they try to teach them? Probably not. However, they will always remember who and what their parents are.

Stay true to our conscious and unconscious minds!

Acceptance Affirmation **Gratitude Poor** Special **Appreciation**
Acknowledgment Talent Thanks

APPRECIATION

Acceptance
   Accept who I am.
   Accept what I have.
   Accept my past (that's what molded me).
   Accept where I am - my present course (that's how and where I get established and move on).

Acknowledgment
   Acknowledge who I am (my strengths, my weaknesses and my areas of improvement).
   Acknowledge my accomplishments (both big and small).
   Acknowledge my failures and learn from them.
   Acknowledge what I lack and work on them.
   Acknowledge what I have and be grateful.
   Acknowledge my cravings to be appreciated.
   Look for opportunities to acknowledge!

Affirmation

Do I care if I do not get an affirmation from others?

When I was insecure and uncertain, I had a tendency to solicit an affirmation.

When I know what I am doing, I am affirming my own actions and beliefs.

To me, affirmation could be a double-edged sword, ie peer support and peer pressure in one package.

Gratitude

There were times I regretted not expressing my gratitude when it was the right thing to do. I am unable to turn back the clock and do the right thing.

I swear to myself that I will not let pride deprive me of expressing gratitude.

Do the right thing and be grateful when it is the right thing to do so!

Poor

Financially poor or lack of materialistic possessions is not the end of the world.

Poor in sympathy and empathy is more detrimental in many aspects.

Special

We are all special in our own way.

No need to compare with others because we are all unique and original.

Most of us have a special someone in our lives.

Appreciate your special someone and appreciate the special YOU!

Talent

We are blessed in different ways.

It takes all kinds of people to make the world.

Ask yourself what talents you have to make your personal and professional worlds a great place to live and work.

Look closer and deeper.

You are a talented person and we are lucky to have you!

Thanks

How often do we express our thanks?

Thanks from our heart will make others feel being appreciated.

Express our thanks in words, writing and gestures.

I used to keep my gratitude to myself and was reluctant to express it.

Over time I realized expressing our thanks in a genuine way should be part of our daily lives.

Thanks tie us together and create a closer bond.

We should not let good deeds be forgotten.

Thanks are not superficial. That's the least I can do to express my gratitude. I feel good after thanking someone who help me out.

Start expressing thanks your own way.

Spread love and thanks!

DREAM

Adventurous
    Get wild.
    Be spontaneous.
    Go with your instinct.
    Believe in yourself.
    You can do it.

I am lucky that I tried many adventures when I was younger. I had the time and resources then, even some did not go well.

If I do not try, doubt will always haunt me on what may happen. Since I tried, regardless of the outcome, I moved on and have no regrets.

Creative

I used to tell myself that "I am a boring person with no creative talents".

As years passed by, I realized most of us have been under-estimating our creative talents.

Believe me, if we look closer, we are creative in many different ways.

For example, it could be the way we write. Nelson often teases my letter 5 and alpha y. To him, my 5 always looks like an 8 while my y reminds him of z.

How about the way we dress?

Some of us could be extremely color-coordinated while some may do mix-and-match to please their own eyes.

When we are at ease, we will be the most creative.

Edge

I will have an in-depth dialogue with myself whenever I need a mental boost.

Go through my strengths and areas for improvement often helps me uncover my edge.

We all have an edge on certain things.

Be proud of our edge and make good use of it.

Uncover your edge today!

Fear
>   What is Fear?
>   False
>   Evidence
>   Appearing
>   Real
>   Now you know how to manage and overcome fear.

Focus
>   Focus requires undivided attention.
>   It connects me with my future.
>   I ask myself why I want to be there and what am I looking.
>   When doubt sets in, I will lose my focus and feel lost.
>   Shake doubt away and remind myself again why and where I want to be.

Freedom
>   Freedom is more than freedom to speak, freedom to act, and freedom to travel.
>   Freedom is to be who I want to be and stay true to myself.
>   I believe everyone should enjoy the freedom to be who they want to be without prejudice.

Hold

I have nice-to-have items on my Hold list. I forgot about my Hold list until I started writing this book.

When I reviewed my Hold list, it shocked me that some of the nice-to-have items are actually important life items that require immediate attention.

When we put things on the back burner, the chances for them to surface again are slim.

Why don't we manage a proactive list on the go and reorganize their priority according to our agenda?

Job

Do you love what you do in a job?

Ask yourself what is right for you.

I made some wrong moves when I did not know what I loved to do. I accepted the first offer that came my way without considering my interests and needs.

During an interview, the candidate is interviewing his/her potential manager as well.

Bear this in mind when you look for your next job.

Be sure to go through what you want to do.

Job is not just about making money.

It is about utilizing your talents to the fullest while you enjoy what you are doing.

It is the only way to do great work.

Motto

My Motto: To be the best of the very best!

Whenever I fall short of my predetermined expectation, I will pause and reflect on why I miss my target.

I treasure the experience, especially the mistakes I made over the years.

Opportunity

Opportunity cost is more important than an opportunity.

What is the difference and why?

Rich

If I am going to be a rich person without a heart and soul, I rather choose to stay poor.

I cherish the richness in knowledge and experience.

Sparkle

Do you notice the sparkle in your eyes?

Enthusiasm and excitement will bring sparkle to our soul and lighten up our eyes.

When our eyes light up with sparkles, we know it is time to showcase our intelligence and share our story with others.

Truthful

Be truthful to myself guides me in my life direction.
I stay focused when I am true to myself.
How about you?

ETIQUETTE

Courtesy
   My biggest pet peeve!
   I believe in incorporating courteous, respectful and considerate manners in our daily lives. For example,
   Wait for one to respond to your "How are you?" before turning away immediately!
   Hold a door for one in need!
   Hold an elevator if one is trying to catch it!
   Bottom Line: Treat others the way you want to be treated.

Cursor

Cursor drives me nuts, especially when it stays on TV/monitor/screen for no reasons.

Most families are using a TV for entertainment and Internet browsing. When the cursor stays on the screen and becomes an eyesore, it is time to move it to a better place.

Eavesdropping

When we are in a public place, those around us are engaged in a private conversation yet they speak loud enough for everyone else in the neighborhood to hear, we are forced to commit an eavesdropping crime.

Do us a favor, please lower your volume so that it will stay as a private chat and not a public speech.

Elevator

I learned this interesting fact from a marketing class.

Mirrors on the walls of elevators are used to keep the passengers entertained.

They help to distract our mind from boredom or fear.

Time flies when we look at our reflection in the mirror thinking.

The waiting does not feel so long when our mind is occupied.

Why is it important to me? I can apply other tricks to engage my audience.

Greeting

It takes two to make a greeting.

Now that we are in a digital world, a personal greeting can be in many different forms.

Regardless of its format, be prompt and respectful when answering a nudge.

Manner

How should we act when we are bombarded with wrongful action and attitude?

I stay firm with the basic manners that one should always be treated with respect.

I am committed not to become bitter regardless of how I will be treated.

Munch

Munch can make me laugh.

Why?

We are often told not to make noise when we eat.

I agree and comply wholeheartedly.

Then when it is inevitable that some food items will make sound on their own, breaking loose is a relief.

We adhere to certain table manners.

However, when we are on our own and are enjoying some casual chats with family and friends, relax and munch loud!

Noise
We are making noise all the time.
Could literally be speaking out loud or having an internal dialogue in our mind.
I learned the hard way to keep things to myself and not to be too revealing.

Please
Such a simple word yet it plays an important role in my life and well-being.

Professional

Why do we want to stay professional?
When will we want to be professional?
Dress and act professionally helps branding for sure.
The question is more about why do we want to be treated professionally?

GROWTH

Ambiguous

I can't help laughing whenever I come across a statement "perform with ambiguity".

To me, ambiguity offers me alternatives because a choice has not been made.

Ambiguity also offers me additional room for exploration and creativity.

There is good and bad ambiguity.

When I am in control, ambiguity could become motivation for me to maneuver.

When I am restrained, ambiguity could choke me.

Answer

Answer and authority often go hand in hand.

How often are you asked to answer a question?

Do you feel powerful when being asked?

Or do you feel intimidated when you do not know the answer?

Saying "I do not know the answer to your question" is an answer on its own.

"Give me some time to think about the answer to your question" is another good answer to a question raised.

Most of us feel intimidated about not being smart enough to come up with a great answer in a timely manner.

Staying truthful and honest is the best answer anyone will appreciate receiving.

Calculative

How do we describe calculative people?

Do we consider ourselves calculative?

Is it good or bad to be calculative?

How about calculating?

Is it better to be calculating than calculative?

Both words come from the same root word.

I have known people who carefully think and plan before making each and every move.

I also have friends inclusive of myself who seldom calculate when leading our lives.

It is your choice and you are always in control!

Change
I prefer to be a change agent to bring along positive changes for better.
Do I welcome change voluntarily?
Most of the time not if I can help it.
I am the type of person who prefers to stay as-is.
My answer may surprise most because I am often seen as a pioneer to be active and proactive in bringing change.
Embrace change!

Choices
I love to have choices in my life.
Don't you?
Having choices means I have to make a decision over multiple options.
I am responsible for the consequences of the option I choose.
There were times when I hoped that someone would make a decision for me.
Having said that, I would still be the one behind the choice because I chose the one to make the decision.
Is it easier or more difficult to choose myself or delegate someone to choose for me?
I don't know.
How about you?

Compare

We have a tendency to compare ourselves with others.

I will make an effort to stop myself when I find I am comparing myself with others.

We are all unique and original.

We are all different.

There is absolutely no way to make objective comparisons of any kind without involving personal prejudice.

When it gets too personal, what is the point of making comparisons?

Agree?

Curiosity

I miss the privilege to ask why whenever and wherever and with whoever.

I learn the most when I can ask why.

When I get older, asking why does not sound right anymore.

I am no different that I want to be smart.

Asking why feels like to disclose my inefficiency that I do not know something.

We are proud in different aspects.

Only until we regain our curiosity and start asking more whys, we may be limiting our growth.

Decision

We have been constantly making decisions or sometimes guesswork on almost everything.

I tried to challenge this statement and failed.

I was going to argue that I am not doing anything. Yet it is already a decision in itself.

Throughout our lives, there are big and small decisions to make.

Sometimes we make a decision on our own.

Sometimes it is a joint decision.

Hopefully most of our decisions have been sensible ones.

There will be times when our decisions are not the smartest and may cost us.

My key learning has been to overcome the hassles my decision has triggered.

Learn not to repeat a bad decision in similar circumstances.

It is fine to make a wrong decision as long as it is not the same mistake.

We cannot make progress without making decisions!

Embrace

Embrace age gracefully.

It is inevitable that we (both people and things) will age over time.

We may as well face the music and age with grace and enjoy the growing process.

Habit
   I have both good and bad habits.
   It takes some willpower to acknowledge their existence and change them.

Hierarchy
   Where are you on the Maslow's Hierarchy of Needs? Why?

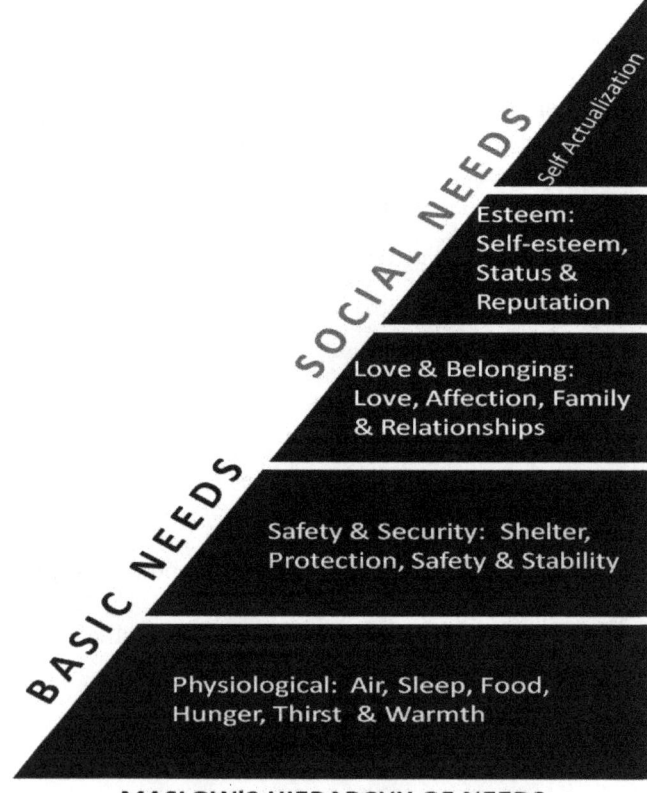

MASLOW'S HIERARCHY OF NEEDS

Humble
　　Stay humble about one's stature.
　　Not many can stay modest and successful after becoming more influential and powerful.
　　I believe in staying humble with dignity, whether I am from a noble background or not.

Image
　　What is your image?
　　Why do you want to maintain and portray your image?
　　Stay fair and respectful is my image.
　　I represent what I stand and believe.
　　I will not bend to please.

Invest
> Invest time on things you want to learn and do.
> Invest in yourself and never look back.
> Invest in relationships and learn from others.
> Invest in your children and their growth will be your return on investment.

Knowledge
> We accumulate knowledge as we learn and grow.
> Are we keeping our knowledge to ourselves?
> Are we willing to share our knowledge?
> Knowledge is meant to be shared so that the society will get richer in every aspect as we evolve from the different stages.

Learning

I am proud to be a learning sponge all my life.

I love to learn and am always open to share.

When we open up to share our learning, the world will be a better place to live.

Think about the benefits and time others will save when we share.

It is the mirror effect.

We learn from others while others learn from us.

The world is round.

It takes all kinds to make the world.

When we are willing to learn and share, we do not need to go through certain growing pains.

Needs

Where are you on the Maslow's Hierarchy of Needs?

For me, Self Actualization where I focus on sharing and giving.

Prepare
Prepare for the worst and hope for the best.
Life is full of surprises and no guaranteed outcomes.
Prepare to look at the positive side from different perspectives.
Life will always be hopeful when we are prepared.

Risk
Risk-taking may mean letting go of old patterns that no longer work.
What is the point of keeping old patterns if they are not working.
It is a gain and not risk.

Temper
I have a temper even though I am a moderate person.
We all have a temper.
Embrace it and accept who we are.
Temper makes us real.
I will not recommend suppression.
Express our temper in a constructive and civil manner.

HAPPINESS

Childhood

The biggest regret in my life has always been missing the chance to create a close bond with my parents and siblings.

My father passed away unexpectedly when I was six.

I have some vague memories with him fetching me home from the kindergarten.

Since my older sister started working when she was 10, I did not spend lots of time with her.

I remembered countable moments with my two young siblings when we played hide-and-seek and shot water guns on cars.

We only have one childhood.

Treasure the time with your parents and siblings!

Chocolate

I am allergic to chocolate.
My skin will start reacting to it if I eat too much.
What is too much?
Two or three small pieces.
There were months I banned chocolate completely from my life.
Then I started consuming one or two occasionally.
Guess what?
I can now eat more than three pieces without substantial allergic reaction.
Chocolate reminds me to be modest.
I will not overdo it!

Clean

I came across an "inner world cleansing" therapy, ie saying the following to myself:
"I love you
I am sorry
Please forgive me
Thank you"
I feel calmer because it reconnects my conscious mind with my subconscious mind.
I am guilty of ignoring my subconscious mind.
I believe my subconscious mind has a better idea of who I want to me!

Modest

Stay modest and humble help me become a better person.

I know where my heart lies when I stay modest.

Boastfulness and great pretensions will prohibit my learning and growth.

R&R

Review and Reflection (R&R) help me grow and mold me into the person I am right now.

R&R will continue helping me to become a better person.

R&R is part of me and I will incorporate R&R into my lifestyle.

Smile
　　Smile is magical.
　　Smile wins us friends.
　　Smile will liven up our lives.
　　Smile will make us look more youthful.
　　Smile will release our tension and grief.
　　Do you know we need over 40 facial muscles to frown and less than 20 facial muscles to smile?
　　Smile more.
　　Share your smile now!

Solitude
　　Solitude helps me shake off my burden and start all over with a clear head.
　　Try it and enjoy solitude!

INSPIRATION

Belief
   We are what we believe in.
   Over time we build confidence and trust in what we believe.
   Our behavior will reflect our beliefs.
   When we are open to believe, belief is our future where we develop ourselves.
   When we have a strong belief in something, couple with desire and intention will manifest into an action.
   Always start with a strong belief!

Blue

Feeling blue is a good thing even it means I am depressed.

According to some scientists, being sad can make us stronger and better to cope with future challenges.

There is nothing wrong to feel blue occasionally.

Once we accept this reality, we are on our way to be more positive in managing our lives.

Branding

We are in a digital world.

Most businesses are talking about creating their brand.

As an individual, what is your brand?

Branding is who you are!

List your values and beliefs.

Validate them with your daily activities and behavior.

If they are consistent and congruent, people will get to see your brand when you are in action.

Commitment
With commitment, my heart is in it.
I have confidence in execution and accomplish the predetermined goal.
That's how I get things done.
Commitment is the first element in everything, even before starting anything.
Remember you are either in or you are out.
In-between does not exist!

Forgetful
Forgetful serves me well because I do not remember what wrongs have been done to me.

Forgiving

Forgiving is a gift that I value in life.

When I have the ability and capacity to forgive, it means I have more than enough to share.

A forgiving heart is the fountain of happiness!

Gain

Tangible or intangible gains.

How and what to quantify gains?

When I am not in red, I am gaining ground.

When I am not backtracking, I am making gains.

When I am staying strong in my current position, I am gathering more strengths to make more gains.

Giver

Having the capacity to give speaks volumes.

I often say "Talk is cheap".

I may not have the physical resources to give.

Yet it does not stop me to give time and share my knowledge and experience.

There is no limit to give our time and share our knowledge.

The more we give away, the more we gain.

It's a win-win.

As a giver, we experience one of life's greatest satisfactions.

Journey

Life is a journey of good and bad times.

We have no idea of its length.

Some are long and some are short.

We have the option to live a fruitful journey with special moments and joys.

We play different roles during different times of our journey.

Without our knowing, our journey may end at the highest note.

Treasure every moment of our journey as if it is going to be the last minute.

We will live our journey with no regret.

Remember: Our life journey begins with the first step!

Life
   Life is a gift.
   I am glad to be here and share what this gift has given me.

Live
   Live to the fullest.
   Why?
   I will only be on this trip once.

Matter

Every step matters.
Every word matters
Every act matters.
What matters most to me has always been staying true to what matters most to me!

Mission

My Mission: Make others' lives easier.
Why?
I cannot change the world and people.
However, I believe I can make positive changes and they may have an impact on the world and people.
I believe in sharing and making differences.

Perfect

I am a perfectionist.

I used to be extremely rigid and everything was either black or white.

It is a shocking surprise that perfect could accommodate imperfect.

Imperfect sometimes supplements perfect if we give it a chance.

Problem

A problem will no longer be a problem if we have a solution or an idea to work on it.

See problems as blessings in disguise!

We are the solution to our problem!

Projection

Project and anticipate how to get to where we want to be.

Projection is an amazing tool to lead and create our future.

Rank

I am at a stage where I am not pursuing a position with a high rank.

Why?

To me, rank does not carry weight.

One's integrity and importance do not come with rank.

One's dedication and attitude to his/her professional life does!

Silence

Silence is golden.

Silence sometimes delivers a message loud and clear.

Try this subtle technique and you will be surprised with its impact.

Strength

Strength ties to willpower.

If there is a will, there will always be ways to get to where we want to be.

Surprise
Life consists of surprises.
That's the beauty of life.
Life will be a bore if we do not get surprised.
Agree?

Taker
I was reluctant to take because I pigheadedly believe in giving unilaterally.

I learned a great lesson when I realized taking actually helped me become a better person.

Think about the pleasure a giver will enjoy when we accept their offer and be a taker.

Giver and Taker complement each other.

We help each other succeed by giving and taking.

Together, we are making the world a safer and gentler place to live.

Be a giver and a taker!

Think
    Are you a thinker or doer?
    My Philosophy: Think hard and work hard!

Uncertainty
    Life is full of uncertainty.
    Uncertainty could be nice and not-so-nice.
    Accept uncertainty helps me move on carefree.

Universe
    I am proud to be part of the Universe.
    I believe in leaving a legacy.
    The life lessons I have learned can leave an extraordinary impact on others.
    You too!
    My life has been touched by others who have come before me.
    It is time to think about what you would like to pass on to others.
    We are all contributors to the Universe!

LOVE

Age
 I have been in my youth paradigm for decades and feel young all the time.
 Age gracefully!

Beauty
 Everything has beauty, but not everyone sees it. Confucius.
 I stayed in an "ugly duckling" spell for years.
 Beauty is reflected in our soul, the way we think, what we do and who we are.
 Beauty is not about external appearance.
 It is more about who and why!

Caring

Caring people have a bigger heart because they feel and exhibit empathy for others.

To be caring is a gift because caring people have the capacity to accommodate others' needs and be there for them.

Caring and Giving often come hand in hand.

Most care and give at the same time.

Family

We are all connected, especially if we happen to be at the same place at the same time.

There are reasons for every encounter.

Where does it lead me?

Be respectful to everyone, even the encounter may only last for some split seconds.

Friend

I am grateful to my friends who have been there for me.

We may not be seeing each other very often.

Whenever I think of my friends, it always brings warmth to me.

It is a good feeling to know that they are out there for me.

We need at least a friend.

I know some consider their pet as their closest friend.

All is good!

Generous

When we are generous in sharing what we have, we are telling the Universe that we are ready to receive more.

When we are sharing, we will be rewarded with more to share.

Being generous will bring us more.

Nothing in our imagination can tell us what may happen.

Gift
   What is the greatest gift in our life?
   Are you prepared to wrap yourself into a gift?

Humane
   Humane is kindness for other beings.
   For example,
   Impoverished people and animals in need of help.
   These kind gestures can be in tangible and intangible forms.

Love
> Love who I am.
> Love what I do.
> Be a loving person in my own way!

Memories
> Memories are stored within us over periods of time.
> Some will fade and become blurred.

The most valuable memories will last forever if we make an effort to preserve them.

Parenthood

When one decides to be a parent, does he/she know parenting is a lifetime commitment?

When I was younger, I was skeptical to parents who expected their children to take care of their materialistic needs (which seemed never-ending and excessive).

When I grew older, I realized my former misunderstanding on parenthood.

Most parents expect nothing in return for their undivided devotion and attention to their children (young and grown alike).

Photos

Those who have known me for years know I was camera shy.

I fled as soon as one suggested taking a shot.

Why did I change?

Photos are the best way to capture and preserve our precious memories.

I recognized this late in my life.

If you have been reluctant to take photos, please act now.

Practice
    Practice makes perfect?
    Not until one practices with passion and diligence.

Siblings
    I have three siblings.
    How would I describe our relationship?
    Close and distant!
    How could close and distant co-exist?
    We have been geographically separated yet we are close in thought.
    I believe there are reasons why we are siblings.
    Treasure this special bond and grow together.

Weight

I had weight issues all my life until I started appreciating my body, regardless of its ups and downs.

I become my own best friend and my own person!

RELATIONSHIP

Attitude
When I heard someone say "She has an attitude", I laughed.
It is a subjective and personal interpretation of another person's expression or behavior.
Before passing a judgment, ask yourself if you may commit the same crime in the past and/or you have the same attitude in yourself.
Last but not least, a positive attitude changes everything and anything!

Attraction
　Like attracts like?
　Opposites attract too?
　Which camp am I in?
　We often make conscious and unconscious choices in our daily lives. For example,
　Favorite color(s)
　Favorite number(s)
　Favorite car(s)
　Favorite people
　Favorite restaurant(s)
　Favorite food
　Favorite actor(s)/actress(es)
　Our favorites do not play a major role in the law of attraction.
　When we love and value ourselves, we will be attracting those who are also positive, open, secure, giving, caring and kind to themselves.

Bonding

Parental bonding

Human bonding

Human-animal bonding

What and how do we bond with our family, friends, children and animals?

Bonding is a mutual and interactive process and is different from liking.

During bonding, emotions such as affection and trust will be developed over time.

Spend quality time together will form a bond.

Challenge

Challenge is good when it encourages me to advance and give my best shot.

Challenge is better when I have someone who has faith in me to accomplish the challenge.

Challenge is the best when I have someone who shares the same belief and we work together to accomplish the challenge.

Challenge won't last forever.

Challenge will make me stronger!

Connect

Mirror pacing and breathing help connecting me with others.

I seldom use this technique in my daily life.

Why?

I notice it is easier to connect with others when I keep an open mind.

I have nothing to hide and do not mind opening up for connection.

I may opt to be on guard for an initial encounter, especially with a stranger.

Trust can be built when one proves to be reliable.

Two may feel a special connection and will connect instantly.

Let's stay open for connection!

Controlling

Controlling is often used to describe a controlling parent or controlling spouse or controlling boss.

We love to defend our autonomy yet we cannot help controlling those under our wings.

I wonder why?

Would it be our nurturing nature to protect or we want to preserve the status quo?

Controlling could be for a good cause.

If not, it's time to rethink and identify a better solution to address our controlling needs.

Credit

Quite often people ask me if I want to be liked or disliked?

My Answer: I prefer to be respected.

I have been working very hard to earn one's respect.

Why?

When we are not adding credits, we could be getting debit.

When we are ourselves and act in the zone, we will be building our credibility automatically.

Entertainment

We need entertainment in our lives.

Life is about work-play balance.

When we find ourselves running out of time enjoying life, pause and regroup.

What is the point of making millions when we do not have minutes to ourselves?

I came across an e-bulletin note suggesting "Take 10 minutes out of each day to clear our mind".

Give it a try and will do us good!

Fair
    Play fair!
    Behave honestly and obey the rules (applicable to both subtle and explicitly written ones).

Favoritism
    There are occasions with overlapping priorities.
    We make our choice to go with who and what with a why behind our decision.
    Does favoritism get in?
    Yes, no or probably.
    Does it mean that we are prejudiced?
    Only if we end up giving unfair preferential treatment to a person at the expense of another.
    Favoritism is unfortunately part of our daily lives.
    When favoritism did injustice to me, I accepted the reality and moved on.
    It is fruitless to linger and I would choose to shake it off.

Jealousy
> Jealousy is inefficiency.
> Jealousy is insecurity.
> When I am content with what I have and who I am, I admire others wholeheartedly.
> Start counting our own blessings.
> There is nothing to be jealous about!

Loss
> The saddest thing I experienced was losing myself in a relationship where I lost my identity.

Reconcile

When and why we choose to reconcile?
If it is a right thing to do, I would patch up with others.
Now you may ask me what is the right thing?
The ball is back in your court.
I would like to know why you think it is the right thing to do.

Respect

Respect is the most important principle in my life dictionary.
Why?
To be respectful is the why to justify my existence.
If one day I am not respectful, I will no longer be myself.
I am very serious about this declaration.

Roles

We wear multiple roles all the time.

The secret is to manage them well and know why we choose to wear them.

For example,

When we choose to stay strong, we must have reasons to believe in ourselves and lead.

When we choose to stay low, we must have reasons to take a break and recuperate.

Acknowledge who we are and the logics behind our decision, we will be content in whatever roles we choose to assume.

Secret

There are good and bad secrets.

Good secrets are meant to be kept for legitimate reasons.

Bad secrets are meant to destroy and hurt.

If we have secrets, be sure to keep the good ones.

TIME

Future
    Worrying about the future is a nuisance.
    No one can foretell for sure what will happen.
    Planning for the future is good.
    Things could turn out to be better or worse.
    Enjoy the process to get to the future is the best life strategy.

Past
    I treasure my past (good and bad).
    I learn from my past (success and failure).
    I value my past, especially the mistakes I made.
    My past has been helping me to get closer to who I want to be.

Present

Live the present moment.

Sometimes it is challenging to manage a present moment.

Actually, we can never grasp a present moment.

As soon as we say it is present, it becomes the past.

How to live the present moment?

When I am content with who I am, what I have and where I am, I am living the present moment.

I have faith and confidence that challenges will bring me to a higher level.

I look forward to making every present moment an interesting and memorable one.

Concentrate my mind on the present moment!

Listen

I am not a good listener.

Most of us are in the same boat.

We are genetically programmed poor listeners because of the gap between the speaking and listening rates.

The average person talks at a rate of about 125-175 words per minute, while we can listen at the rate of up to 450 words per minute.

With this 75% differential, our minds have a tendency to wander.

The good news is we can all be trained to become a better listener.

How?

Make an effort to stay tuned in to the speaker.

Patience

Patience is the ability to keep a positive attitude while waiting.

All good things are worth waiting for and worth fighting for.

Pause

I was a workaholic and seldom paused.

I thought I could work endlessly and restlessly forever.

The truth is "pause is an energizer".

Pause gives me room to regroup and be more effective.

Start cushioning pauses in your life and you will be amazed!

Punctual

I feel guilty if I'm running late for a meeting or an appointment, especially when the group is over two (not just with me).

Why?

It is bad enough to be late for a meeting with another person.

When the party involves over two, I cannot get over the time wasted while waiting for me.

Please be punctual!

Retirement

Retirement has not been on my mind.

Not because I am too young to think about it.

I have friends who retire and yet their retirement lifestyle has been more occupied than their working lives.

Retirement does not exist if we are mentally and physically attached to excessive business activities.

One day when and if I retire, I will be a free agent with no attachment.

Sensible

I urge my friends and customers to make sensible decisions.

Sense (mind) plus able (being) - use both our head and heart to make a decision!

Talk it out helps too.

When it does not sound right, it is not sensible.

When it does not feel right, it is not sensible.

When we do not have the resources to do it right, it is not sensible.

Timing
  Timing is everything - so TRUE!

WELLNESS

Anger

Anger is our emotional response when we feel threatened.

If we use anger for a constructive purpose, it is a different story.

Only when anger becomes uncontrollable or in some circumstances unexpressed, it may lead to destructive behavior.

I believe anger is healthy for us to express our feelings. It is completely normal.

Audio

I recommend all of us participate in "Reduce Unwanted Noise".

Why?

There are bylaws that we will get a fine for disturbing the neighborhood.

It is a legitimate reason, though the following should seal the deal.

For our auditory health care please.

Noise exposure can cause two kinds of health effects, namely

Non-auditory Effects: Stress, safety and physiological and behavioral effects.

Auditory Effects: Hearing impairment.

Balance

What have I been doing to balance my mental, emotional and physical health?

Thinking (Mental)
Smiling (Emotional)
Walking (Physical)
What is your balance technique?

Basics

According to Maslow's Hierarchy of Needs, our basic needs include physiological, safety and security ones.

Physiological: Air, sleep, food, hunger, thirst and warmth.

Safety & Security: Shelter, protection, safety and stability.

I admire those volunteering their time and resources to get the basic needs to those in need.

Breathe

Take a deep breath everyone.

Do you know how to inhale and exhale?

Surprisingly, I do not remember breathing most of the time.

I am a very tense person and often stress myself unnecessarily.

When it comes to coping with stress overload, our breathing is one of the best remedies and it's free!

When we feel a little depressed or anxious or tired, our breathing has amazing healing powers.

Knowing How to Breathe: Inhale, exhale, relax and energize!

Watch and expand our breathing for some minutes.

Notice the positive impact on our energy level and mood.

It works!

Clutter

It bothers me whenever I feel trapped in a clutter.

There were times I tried too hard to free myself and ended up double-trapped in a clutter.

When I am prepared to stay in a clutter for a while, I start seeing new perspectives.

It is a relief to regain control and everything back to normal.

Stay positive when we try to sort things out.

Give ourselves time and space when we are in a clutter.

Control

Control is a demanding word.

I am not interested in controlling others.

I would like to be in control of my life.

Life is more interesting (whether we agree or not) if there are puzzles to be solved.

When we know what is going to happen, quite often the certainty will spoil for us.

Cry

When I was younger, I used to hide and cry my heart out.

When I get older, I have not been crying as much.

Is it good or bad?

There is nothing wrong with crying.

When our emotion explodes and needs to release out of our body, crying will soothe and bring us back to balance.

Suppression is not good for our mental health.

I admire those who feel free to express and release their emotions.

I believe all of us have the right to enjoy the freedom to laugh and cry as we please.

Crying does not necessarily mean that we are sad.

We can cry when we are excited and filled with joy.

When I am angry, crying is a good way to release my frustration.

It is a natural way to feel better and that matters!

Doubt

I do not want to be in doubt.

It is a dark place to be surrounded by uncertainty and fear.

How do I manage doubts?

Stay in a positive mindset.

Just take one small step at a time.

How about having doubts about others or a venture?

I usually map out what needs to be addressed, what do we want to accomplish, and how to get to where we want. With consensus and commitment as a team, focus on specific steps to get there.

When our energy and efforts are spent on why, we are in a better position to figure out how and what we need to get there.

Once we have a clear picture, doubts disappear!

Emotion

Emotion is our closest ally.

It is a subjective experience that no words can describe how we feel at a certain point of time and situation.

Emotion could be reacting to an internal or external event.

If it is reactive, how could emotion be subjective?

Emotion could be planted if we expect consistent responses to a predetermined series of events.

Materialistic achievements and objects can impact our emotion as well.

What does it lead us to?

Stay alert to being stirred up.

Respect our instinct and respond to internal or external stimuli naturally.

If we don't, we will become a robot that is programmed to respond in a consistent manner.

It is sad because we should be free to react and respond the way we want to.

Flexible

To be flexible without breaking.

To be capable of adjusting easily without twisting the truth or bending toward the wrong.

I am flexible though I am not afraid of telling the truth and sharing my opinion.

I stay true to myself and belief, though I am flexible to listen to other's opinion.

I am flexible and not judgmental.

Health

Mental health = our mind

Physical health = our body

How well have you been taking care of your mind and body?

It is time to do an inventory check and make changes to get our mental and physical health to the next level!

Laugh

    Laugh livens up our spirit.

    Laugh makes us look more youthful.

    Laughing also brings us health benefits such as lowering blood pressure and heart rate.

    We do not need a reason to laugh.

    Laugh when we feel like having a good laugh!

Mental

    Staying mentally fit and healthy is the number one priority item on my list.

    It worths spending time to find resources that I can do on a regular basis to maintain my mental health.

Retreat

I was fortunate to attend a foundational conference in Phoenix facilitated by Brugh Joy.

Brugh was an inspirational leader with passion and vision.

With Brugh's guidance, I was able to connect with my subconscious mind.

I appreciated Brugh's sharing his story of the spiritual transformation and had glimpses of my own healing power.

Most retreats offer a positive and supportive learning environment for the attendees to share and learn.

I encourage you to step out of your comfort zone and give it a try!

Learn -> Unlearn -> Relearn

Sleep

We all need our beauty and handsome sleep.

I am not a heavy sleeper.

I crave for a peaceful sleep at night.

Sleep is where I find peace and comfort.

Wealth

Mental wealth vs physical wealth - what is my choice if I can only pick one?

I would go with mental wealth because it means a meaningful life experience.

There is no shortcut in developing our mental wealth.

Very often our mental wealth grows one wisdom at a time.

What is your pick?

Worry

I was a worrywart and worried about everything.

It was not a surprise when I learned that worrying could be a technique I created to fill the moments of my life.

It sounds outrageous.

It has some truth to it.

Stop worrying and instead focus on what you have to gain!

CORE VALUES

5Cs
   I am proud of my 5Cs.
   They are as good as the 5Cs to assess diamonds.
   Compassion
   Competence
   Commitment
   Communication
   Crisp

5Rs
   I also cherish my 5Rs as they align with my values.
   Reliable
   Resourceful
   Respective
   Responsible
   Responsive

KISS
  Keep
  It
  Simple and
  Stupid

  Keep
  It
  Short and
  Sweet

I+U or U+I
  I or You should come first?
  It depends on the circumstances.
  My guideline has been putting myself in your place and seeing how I feel.
  When I am assessing myself, the focus will be on I with every intention to realize better differences on a similar situation in the future.
  Regardless of You or I, I am responsible for the experience.

PIN

PIN helps me lead my life with a positive note.
Start with Positive.
Continue with Interesting.
End with Negative only if I still want to go through it.
Very often no!
Why do I always start with Positive?
If I stay positive, I believe good things and good people will be drawn to me.

SMART

SMART has been keeping me on track.
I cannot live without SMART, especially my life goals.
Specific
Measurable
Achievable
Realistic
Time bound

Ws
> Start with Why.
> Continue with hoW and What.
> Name the Who.
> Specify When and Where.
>
> Why do I start with Why?
> Why is the catalyst.
> Why helps me understand why I do what I do.
> hoW helps me reflect how I do what I do.
> Then I know what I do.

BIOGRAPHY

Beth is a dynamic lady with extensive life experience in both Eastern and Western environments. She has lived and worked in three international cities (Beijing, Hong Kong and Toronto) and travelled extensively across 15+ countries (over 100 cities).

She has gained substantial insight into different organizational cultures and management practices from her various management positions and consultation projects. For example,

-General Manager
 Fleming International Limited
 Hong Kong and Shenzhen, PR China
-Assistant Vice President, Operations Management
 AIG Finance (Hong Kong) Limited, Hong Kong
-Senior Credit Administrator
 Swiss Bank Corporation (Canada), Toronto, Canada
-Employee Development
 Scotia Capital, Toronto, Canada
-Office Manager
 WJS International Inc, Beijing, PR China

Beth fell in love with training after years of Toastmasters learning. Her starting a consulting and soft skills training business (= leaving a senior management position with AIG) had surprised a lot of people.

Beth has touched thousands of lives on a global basis. She inspired hundreds of people to become a public speaking member. She was the owner and organizer of a multi-million HK$ Christmas function.

Her quality leadership and passion have attracted lots of media attention. Beth was interviewed by AlterMedic.com, Hamilton Spectator (a local newspaper in the Halton Region, Ontario, Canada), Metro Broadcast Hong Kong, Toronto CBCC, and The Record (a local newspaper of the Kitchener/Waterloo region in Ontario Canada). Stories about her vision were reported in Hamilton Spectator, The Record, Oriental Daily, Apple Daily, Hong Kong Economic Times, The Sun, Sing Tao Daily, Ming Pao, Central Magazine, Eat & Travel, and Sisters. Her most recent media appearances were on the CBC Dragons' Den (Toronto), Seasons VIII and IX.

Beth is known for her big heart in sharing. She has a strong passion of helping others excel!

Professional Accomplishments

Area Governor of the Year, Toastmasters International, Pan-Southeast Asia Pacific Region

Distinguished Toastmaster (DTM), Toastmasters International, Hong Kong Division

Distinguished President's Area Award, Toastmasters International USA

Co-chair of the First District Toastmasters Convention in Hong Kong, Toastmasters International, Pan-Southeast Asia Pacific Region

Champion of an Inter-club Evaluation Contest, Toastmasters International, Hong Kong

Designer/Facilitator of over 150 Experiential Training Programs, Facilitation Sessions and Speaking Assignments (Canada, China PRC, Macau, Pan-Southeast Asia Pacific Region, Saudi Arabia, Taiwan ROC, The Philippines and USA)

Organizer/Advisor of over 200 Public and Private Functions (up to 7,000 participants) (Canada, China PRC, Macau, Pan-Southeast Asia Pacific Region, Taiwan ROC, Thailand, The Philippines and USA)

Academic Accomplishments

Bachelor of Applied Arts (Hons)
School of Administration and Information Management
Ryerson University, Toronto, Canada

Diploma in Adult Training and Development
University of Toronto, Toronto, Canada

Certified Social Media Strategist
Social Media Marketing University, USA

Certificates in Teaching English to Speakers of Other Languages (TESOL)
TESL, Ottawa, Canada
Trinity College London, England

Canadian Securities Course (Hons)
The Canadian Securities Institute, Toronto, Canada

Diploma in Multimedia Web Site Design
Unisoft Education Center, Hong Kong

http://www.bethfiedler.com
http://www.wp-winpro.weebly.com

GLOSSARIES

5Cs	79	Decision	21
5Rs	79	Doubt	72
Acceptance	1	Dream	5
Acknowledgment	1	Eavesdropping	12
Adventurous	5	Edge	6
Affirmation	2	Elevator	13
Age	43	Embrace	21
Ambiguous	17	Emotion	73
Anger	67	Entertainment	55
Answer	18	Etiquette	11
Appreciation	1	Fair	56
Attitude	51	Family	44
Attraction	52	Favoritism	56
Audio	68	Fear	7
Balance	68	Flexible	74
Basics	69	Focus	7
Beauty	43	Forgetful	33
Belief	31	Forgiving	34
Blue	32	Freedom	7
Bonding	53	Friend	45
Branding	32	Future	61
Breathe	69	Gain	34
Calculative	18	Generous	45
Caring	44	Giver	35
Challenge	53	Gift	46
Change	19	Gratitude	2
Childhood	27	Greeting	13
Chocolate	28	Growth	17
Choices	19	Habit	22
Clean	28	Happiness	27
Clutter	70	Health	74
Commitment	33	Hierarchy	22
Compare	20	Hold	8
Connect	54	Humane	46
Control	70	Humble	23
Controlling	54	I+U	80
Courtesy	11	Image	23
Creative	6	Inspiration	31
Credit	55	Invest	24
Cry	71	Jealousy	57
Curiosity	20	Job	8
Cursor	12	Journey	35

Knowledge	24	Rank	39
Laugh	75	Reconcile	58
Learning	25	Relationship	51
Life	36	Respect	58
KISS	80	Retirement	64
Listen	62	Retreat	76
Live	36	Rich	9
Loss	57	Risk	26
Love	47	Roles	59
Manner	14	R&R	29
Matter	37	Secret	60
Memories	47	Sensible	65
Mental	75	Sibling	49
Mission	37	Silence	40
Modest	29	Sleep	76
Motto	9	SMART	81
Munch	14	Smile	30
Needs	25	Solitude	30
Noise	15	Sparkle	10
Opportunity	9	Special	3
Parenthood	48	Strength	40
Past	61	Surprise	41
Patience	63	Taker	41
Pause	63	Talent	4
Perfect	38	Temper	26
Photos	48	Thanks	4
PIN	81	Think	42
Please	15	Time	61
Poor	3	Timing	66
Practice	49	Truthful	10
Prepare	26	U+I	80
Present	62	Uncertainty	42
Problem	38	Universe	42
Projection	39	Ws	82
Professional	16	Wealth	77
Punctual	64	Weight	50
		Wellness	67
		Worry	78

- End -

www.ingramcontent.com/pod-product-compliance
Lightning Source LLC
Chambersburg PA
CBHW031449040426
42444CB00007B/1028